TRANQUILITY
TRANSFORMATION
TRANSCENDENCE

LOW-QUALITY PRINT SAMPLE

TRANQUILITY
TRANSFORMATION
TRANSCENDENCE
The Enchanting Promises
of Public Gardens

Featuring
CANTIGNY PARK, THE MORTON ARBORETUM,
CHICAGO BOTANIC GARDEN

Mary K. Doyle

TRANQUILITY TRANSFORMATION TRANSCENDENCE
The Enchanting Promises of Public Gardens

Mary K. Doyle

Edited by Gregory F. Augustine Pierce
Designed and typeset by Andrea Reider
Photographs by Mary K. Doyle

Library of Congress Catalog number: 2023935340
ISBN: 978-0-87946-726-5
Printed in the United States of America by Total Printing Systems
Year 30 29 28 27 26 25 24 23
Printing 10 9 8 7 6 5 4 3 2 First
Text printed on 70# 30%-post-consumer-recycled paper

Contents

INTRODUCTION

Three Public Gardens,
One Poet/Photographer

Like wine and cheese or baseball and statistics or kids and slides, poetry and nature pair perfectly. Emotional and sensual, they prompt joy, contemplation, and intrigue.

When we walk through nature, all our senses come alive. How can we not enjoy the fragrance of spring blossoms, summer wind gently tussling our hair, the rustling of leaves in the fall, or the crunch of the winter earth beneath our feet?

We react to poetry in a similar way. At their best, poems warm or pain our hearts. Poetic rhythm is soulful. We are affected by the words and images on multiple human levels. And, like nature, every bit of a poem — every syllable, every breath, every image or metaphor is to be taken in slowly and savored. The result is exhilarating…yet contemplative.

The poems in this book were inspired by photos captured by me at three public gardens, all in the Chicago suburbs: Cantigny Park in Wheaton, The Morton Arboretum in Lisle, and the Chicago Botanic Garden in Glencoe. Why these three? First of all, they are near where I live now and have lived my entire life. Second, all three provide a transformative experience to visitors who come once in a lifetime or once every few weeks or months. Third, they all have admissions policies that offer discounts or free admissions on special days or events, food and drink services, and gift-shop purchases. (Some organizations also have reciprocal membership admission policies with similar venues. That is something you may want to investigate with all public gardens or arboreta you visit in North America.)

Venture into one of these magnificent nature preserves, or a similar-quality one near you, and you will feel as if you've left the busy, challenging, or confusing world behind. A bit of Paradise-on-Earth awaits. The colors of the seasons are revealed in each of these three public parks through themed gardens, nature walks, horticultural programs, special events, picnic areas, playgrounds, gift shops, and educational classes.

Cantigny Park is located on the former estate of Colonel Robert R. McCormick in Wheaton, Illinois, straight west of Chicago on Roosevelt Road. The public grounds consist of 500 acres of stunning formal and informal gardens including the rose garden, octagon garden, fountain garden, rock and gravel gardens, and idea garden in addition to wooded areas, a 27-hole golf course, and restaurants. Visitors also may enjoy the nature walks, picnic areas, playground, and the First Division Museum and garden where guests can explore military tanks from World War I through Desert Storm.

The Morton Arboretum in Lisle, Illinois, sits on 1,700 acres just off I-88 and state Route 53. It features an abundance of a variety of trees in collections and natural areas, an award-winning children's garden, a maze garden, four seasons garden, fragrance garden, and 16 miles of trails for hiking and nine miles of roads for biking and driving. The Morton Arboretum also offers programs, events, and exhibitions that connect guests with trees and nature for learning and enjoyment. The arboretum grounds are open 365 days a year.

The Chicago Botanic Garden in Glencoe, Illinois, is off I-94 at Lake Cook Road near Highland Park and features nine islands, twenty-seven different gardens, four natural areas, and a bell clarion on 385 acres. Visitors can take advantage of the renowned bonsai collection, heritage garden, native plant garden, sensory garden, and English Walled Garden, in addition to the Model Railroad Garden, the Grand Tram Tours, musical performances, and a variety of special events. Owned by the Forest Preserve District of Cook County and operated by the Chicago Horticultural Society, the Chicago Botanic Garden is open every day of the year.

My many photos from these beautiful public parks moved me to write the accompanying poems in a particular way, both in content and form. I could have responded to some of the pictures in several directions, while others shouted out to me very specifically. You will find the poems covering a variety of topics and include haiku, cinquain, and free verse.

Throughout it all, my work producing this book for you was delightful for me. Every moment of photography, writing, editing, and rewriting, rewriting, and rewriting was uplifting and inspiring. It is my hope and my prayer (and I mean that literally) that viewing these photos and reading these poems will be uplifting and inspiring for you as well. I bid you peace and joy.

Mary K. Doyle
Batavia, Illinois

Redbud ◆ Spring ◆ The Morton Arboretum

Natural Beauty

Beauty doesn't have to be expensive.
Glance out the window.
Walk through a public garden.
Look at clouds, greenery, wildlife.
Nature offers us the most
fragrant, aesthetically pleasing,
and texturally interesting sites
we can possibly hope to see.
Truly tranquil.
Truly transformative.
Truly transcendent.

Daffodil heads ✦ Spring ✦ Cantigny Park

Delicate

Delicate petals

daintily floating toward me.

Fragrant gift of spring.

Waterlily ◆ Spring ◆ Chicago Botanic Garden

Like a Waterlily

I wish I could
sit alone,
out on a lush bed of leaves,
basking in the warm sunshine,
surrounded by peaceful waters

where I could
comfortably meditate
on past events,
creative projects,
and a fulfilling future.

Russian sage, fountain grass ✦ Summer ✦ Cantigny Park

The Natural Flow

Go with the natural flow
even when it takes you
in seemingly senseless directions—
first this, then that crazy way—
yet soon you learn
the importance
and purpose of it all.

Pinecones ✦ Summer ✦ The Morton Arboretum

Conifer Decor

Once, a dinosaur delicacy
and now treats for squirrels and birds,
cones are environmental indicators
that adorn conifers like ornaments.

Cones close scales to protect seeds
from biting cold, wind, and invaders
and open when it is safe for them
to release precious seeds ready to germinate.

Simple beauty. Beautifully functional.

Roses ✦ Spring ✦ Chicago Botanic Garden

Hold Me Close

Hold me close,
my love,
so close together
our hearts
beat as one,
so close together
our hearts
are one.

Malay lacewing butterfly ◆ Summer (Butterflies and
Blooms Exhibit) ◆ Chicago Botanic Garden

Top Place

President and CEO.
Senior Manager.
Administrator.

It's not only how we get to the top
but also, what we do while there . . .
and knowing when to step away.

Coleus, marigolds, zinnias ◆ Autumn ◆ Cantigny Park

Autumn Pop

Autumn colors pop

like fizzy, fruity sodas

tingling our senses.

Trees, foliage ✦ Autumn ✦ The Morton Arboretum

How We Process

Our environment impacts us in different ways.
Some of us are more sensitive than others
to storms or showers, floods or drought,
wind gusts or breezes, sunshine or shade,
and steamy or frigid temperatures.

The true colors of our being are revealed
in how we process what comes our way,
where we firmly hold our ground,
when we struggle or succeed,
how we matured into who we are today.

Petunias ✦ Spring ✦ Chicago Botanic Garden

You're Not Alone

What was below, is above.

What was above, is below.

When the world seems upside down,
look up for showers of flowers
gently falling from heaven,
showers of love
raining down on you.

Evergreens ✦ Winter ✦ Cantigny Park

Beneath the White Blanket

In the evergreen forest
sprays of red and brown
strategically dot the fluffy powder
like the tucks on a quilt.

What secrets hide beneath
that blanket of snow?
What will we find
when it melts away?

Freeman maple tree ✦ Summer ✦ The Morton Arboretum

Power of Being

With age comes courage.

We dig in and brace ourselves.

It's the power of being.

New England asters ✦ Autumn ✦ Cantigny Park

Vivid Fuchsia Faces

Vivid fuchsia faces
smiling bright and happy
wide awake in the autumn wind.

A timely remembrance
of the royal treasures
generously present each season.

Gladiator onion ✦ Spring ✦ Chicago Botanic Garden

Celebrating You

Celebrating you.

A festive spray of fireworks

shooting for your dreams.

Great blue heron ◆ Spring ◆ The Morton Arboretum

Persistent Payoff

Curious
Great blue heron
searching for treasures
along the stream's lush bank.

Persistent
inquisition
drawing you
into corners and crevices.

Rewarded
for your efforts
of patient hunting
with prized delicacies.

Landscape ✦ Spring ✦ Chicago Botanic Garden

We Connect

We connect
like the flow of landscape
from one to another—
one person,
one community,
one country,
one world.

Hand-in-hand
complimenting one another
layer-upon-layer
enhancing,
(also detracting),
for the good of all.

Mums, marigold, grasses ✦ Autumn ✦ Cantigny Park

Like Sunset

Like sun setting on the horizon
in its daily departure from sight,
chrysanthemum colors dazzle
in descending autumn shades
from lemon yellow to burnt rust.

Black-eyed Susans ✦ Summer ✦ The Morton Arboretum

Sunny Susans

Bumble bees flocking

to a sunny Susan field.

Sure sign of summer.

Lily pads, mosaic plant ✦ Summer ✦ Chicago Botanic Garden

Beautiful Differences

True beauty is found

in our differences

and similarities

Easter Basket roses ♦ Autumn ♦ Cantigny Park

Easter Basket Roses

Easter Basket roses
blooming in November.
Light, delicate, fragrant.

A blush of pink, sweet cream,
and buttery yellow.
A kiss from summer past.

Flowering trees ✦ Spring ✦ The Morton Arboretum

Listen to the Wind

Listen to the wind and the tales she tells.
She knows the secrets of love, joy, and loss.

Always on the move, traveling north to south,
south to north, east to west, and back.

Rattling the windows. Rustling through the trees.
Gliding by, dancing, swirling, and spinning.

Whispering stories of things seen and heard.
Carrying kisses blown into the wind.

Eastern red cedar ✦ Autumn ✦ Cantigny Park

Cedar Cones

Eastern red cedar,
evergreen cypress
with hardy, adaptable, scale-like needles.

Bedecked in late summer-fall
with blue-green, berry-like, modified-cones.
Attractive delicacies for the birds.

Tree roots near water ✦ Spring ✦ Chicago Botanic Garden

Knuckle Down

I proudly show my rough knuckles
from when I rooted in
against the turbulent water
against the biting wind.

I stand stronger from the hardships
and what I have endured
with comfort in my weathered skin
with foundation secured.

Tulips, daffodils ✦ Spring ✦ The Morton Arboretum

Spring

The awakening
of tulips in bloom.

The morning love song
of doves in chorus.

The light, fragrant whiff
of bright hyacinths.

The gentle caress
of fresh, warm breezes.

The vibrant colors
of young life anew.

Fish pond ◆ Autumn ◆ Cantigny Park

Fish Flowing Freely

Fish flowing freely
swimming, swirling
gracefully gliding
circling slowly
around and among.

Enabling Garden ◆ Spring ◆ Chicago Botanic Garden

Content or Curious?

In which direction are you drawn the most—
the abundant foliage in the garden,
or what's possible beyond the pathway?

The rich bounty within is obvious.
The gifts, or losses, outside are unknown.
So—are you more content or curious?

Greenery along Lake Marmo ✦ Summer ✦ The Morton Arboretum

Power of Green

Nature provides rich benefits
with its powerful greenery—
plant-life vital to our survival.

What else
filters odors,
reduces stress,
speeds healing,
increases humidity,
improves air quality,
aids attention deficit,
boosts productivity, and
connects us to our planet?

Bullfrog ✦ Spring ✦ The Morton Arboretum

I See You

Looking at me
while I look at you
wide-eyed,
still,
quiet,
curious.

Shoreline along the lake ✦ Summer ✦ Chicago Botanic Garden

Steward of All Living Things

I believe in a God who made me
as an integral element of creation,
as a steward of all living things,
from the smallest particles to the largest.

I am a beneficiary
of this dynamic and diverse environment
and therefore fully responsible
for its continued growth, health, and well-being.

Lamb's ear ✦ Spring ✦ Cantigny Park

Soft as a Lamb's Ear

Sweet baby,
with skin as silky as a young lamb's ear
and milky perfume
in the folds of your neck,

I nuzzle
into your cuddly adorableness
while your pudgy little hand
grasps my finger.

Monarch butterfly on phlox ✦ Summer ✦ Cantigny Park

The Royal Monarch

A delicate beauty,
the royal butterfly
samples sweet nectar,
nature's fuel,
to continue its part
in the tag-team life-cycle
of a highly-evolved migration.

Orchids ✦ Winter (Orchid Show) ✦ Chicago Botanic Garden

Yearning for Spring

Yearning for spring to return,
indoor blooms
bend toward the light
with a burst of faith
and the signal of rebirth.

Lake Marmo ✦ Spring ✦ The Morton Arboretum

Like Silver

So unpretentious.
But then, here you are,
solid, reliable, dependable.

Like your shimmering, silvery shadow,
your presence is a precious gift to me.

Smoke tree ✦ Spring ✦ Cantigny Park

Seek the Less Obvious

Center stage is crowded.

The actors, jugglers, and magicians
feed on our attention
while the less obvious guests fade
into the smokey back room.

Treasures are only found
by those who follow the clues.

Great blue heron ♦ Spring ♦ Chicago Botanic Garden

Queen Heron

Regal Queen Heron

with elegant, graceful curves

and royal stature.

Lake Marmo ✦ Spring ✦ The Morton Arboretum

God's Paint Brush

Nature's sweeping brush

paints watercolor highlights

across the landscape.

Roses ✦ Spring ✦ Cantigny Park

One with the Wallflowers

Like a wall of flowers,
tightly bound,
we grow stronger
by leaning on others.

We're no longer alone.
We reach for the sun
and soak in the raindrops
blossoming together.

Pond slider turtle ✦ Spring ✦ The Morton Arboretum

Move Onward

Look up
when life is tough
and mud draws you under.
Pull yourself out of it
and move onward.

Zinnias, echinacea ◆ Summer ◆ Chicago Botanic Garden

Happiest

I'm happiest outside

surrounded by greenery,
blossoms, and butterflies,

enveloped in the warmth of sunshine
and brushed by cool, gentle breezes,

listening to the rustle of leaves
and chatter of birds,

and enticed by the sweet
fragrance of flowers in bloom.

Bank of Lake Marmo ◆ Spring ◆ The Morton Arboretum

Cheers to the Mentor

Cheers to the mentor

who reaches down to promote

those aiming upwards.

Roses ✦ Spring ✦ Chicago Botanic Garden

Rose Party

Roses preparing for festivities,
a party for their guests.
Like frosting flowers on a birthday cake,
they're a sweet, creamy pink.

Roses begin by emitting their fragrance
as their grand invitation
and opening wide to welcome guests
of sunrays, raindrops, and bees.

The party begins around the stigma,
petals gathering there,
spiraling out, one after another,
dancing toward emerald leaves.

Cardinal ◆ Spring ◆ Cantigny Park

No Hiding a Cardinal

No hiding for you

from a world that loves your song

and your brilliant coat.

Clematis on a tree ✦ Spring ✦ Chicago Botanic Garden

Dressed in Clematis

Posed like a model.

Smartly dressed in clematis

with a flowing train.

Gold Pond ✦ Summer ✦ Cantigny Park

When Heaven Speaks

In the moments between sleep and awake,
the time when heaven speaks,
all is well.

Love radiates.
Beauty blossoms.
Peace sings.

Wooded path ◆ Spring ◆ The Morton Arboretum

Sit with Me

My friend,
please, sit and rest.
I really want to know
how you are feeling.
You are special to me.

Salvia, zinnias ✦ Summer ✦ Cantigny Park

In the Light

We can't appreciate,
or fully understand,
the entire story
until all comes to light.

Copper beech tree ✦ Spring ✦ The Morton Arboretum

Copper Beech Tree Trunk

Sir Copper Beech Tree,
your trunk makes me smile.
You are like an elephant creature
with displaced eyes
and mammoth, mis-sized feet.

May I sit and rest
in the cool, dark shade
under your protective, outstretched arms?
I am intrigued
by your unique presence.

Dried hydrangeas ✦ Winter ✦ Chicago Botanic Garden

White Winter Days

Dried hydrangeas
swaying on a bed
of new-fallen snow
celebrating the season.

The glory of the
clean and crisp
bright and brisk
white winter days.

Dragonfly ✦ Summer ✦ The Morton Arboretum

Dragonfly

Speedy dragonfly
zooms across the murky pond,
then abruptly lands
on a cluster of berries.

All life requires
a balance of nourishment,
exercise, and rest
before taking off again.

Orchids ♦ Winter (Orchid Show) ♦ Chicago Botanic Garden

Wake Up

Energetic yellow faces
with open ruby lips
calling in unison...

"Wake up!
Look up!
Stand up!"

...for what is good,
what matters,
what is needed.

House sparrow ✦ Spring ✦ Cantigny Park

Please Answer Me

Hello!
Do you hear me?
I'm singing my best song,
and not one bird is responding.
Frustrating!

Stream between Sterling Pond and Lake Marmo
✦ Summer ✦ The Morton Arboretum

Called to Follow

Pathways and rivers call to me,
a call so powerful I'm lured in
and follow in search of a magical world
that intertwines reality and fantasy.

In my perfect place,
warm breezes enfold me like my favorite blanket,
sunlight dazzles like pure diamonds,
and flora and fauna represent the rainbow.

The kind residents welcome me as one
in this haven where everything is loved,
everything is honored,
everything is appreciated.

A dreamland where possibilities are endless.

Waterlilies ◆ Spring ◆ Chicago Botanic Gardens

Closeness of Friends

Some people are like the lilies of the pond
who enjoy the nearness of friends,
inviting each other to join in,
resting closely to the next,
opening their faces to the sun,
and reflecting their joy outward.

Grasses ✦ Autumn ✦ Cantigny Park

Spray of Grasses

In a dynamic dance,

sprays of colorful grasses

transition to fall.

Pond ✦ Spring ✦ Chicago Botanic Garden

Who Wears It Best?

Who wears it best—
The blue in the sky or on the water?
The white in the clouds or on the water?
The green in the tree or on the water?

We see these colors
above and below, outside and within,
through still and smooth rapid and wavy dances
proudly parading nature's flag.

Cork tree ✦ Spring ✦ The Morton Arboretum

Wrapped in Your Arms

I am safe and loved

wrapped in your powerful arms.

No harm can touch me.

Evergreens ✦ Winter ✦ Cantigny Park

Cold, Bold Beauty

Winter wonderland
of deep evergreen and stark white.

The dazzling sun marks the snow
with indigo shadows.

Reflections of the season's
vividly intense beauty.

Eranthis hyemalis (commonly called winter aconite)
♦ Winter ♦ Cantigny Park

Hope Is

Hope is the first bloom of spring flowers,
the dawn after a night's storm,
the steady roll of ocean waves,
the stars that shine in the darkest night.

Earth keeps turning,
one day at a time.

Time keeps passing,
one moment at a time.

We keep moving,
one step at a time.

Shimpaku juniper (estimated age 50-60 years)
✦ Summer (Bonsai Collection) ✦ Chicago Botanic Garden

Detour

Sometimes that detour

is the only way to get

where we want to go.

Magnolia ✦ Spring ✦ The Morton Arboretum

Graceful Survivor

Magnolia,
elegant survivor,
since the dawn of creation.
For countless millions of years,
you've graced our planet.

Fragrant,
waxy-looking petals
streaked in shades
of white, pink, purple, green, or yellow
often appear before your leaves.

Bridge over Lake Marmo ✦ Summer ✦ The Morton Arboretum

Embrace the Bridges

Life is a series of transitions—
birth, blossom, decline, and death.
We evolve and grow
throughout and within
a world in constant motion.

Learning to embrace the bridges—
the approaches, crossings, and crossing overs—
helps us to understand and appreciate situations
that provide lessons and opportunities.

Papaver (commonly called poppy) ♦ Spring ♦ Chicago Botanic Garden

Poppy Presentation

Poppy presentation in the park
dusty red against spring green
posing perfectly for our pleasure.

Delicate tissue-paper flowers
topped with festive pistil bows
proudly presented to the public.

Turkey ✦ Autumn ✦ Cantigny Park

Turkey Time

Leaves are turning colors, and fall is here.
Not a turkey's favorite time of year.
From spring to summer, life was great.
Plump from seeds and insects it ate,
it's now the focus of holiday cheer.

Pumpkins, squashes, kale, pansies, mums, Joseph's coat
groundcover ✦ Autumn ✦ Cantigny Park

Autumn Abundance

Root vegetables and kales,
squashes and pumpkins,
tree fruits and nuts.
Autumn abundance
across the fields.

Harvest heartily,
appreciate fully,
store carefully,
for the winter is
long and barren.

Spruce, weeping willow ✦ Summer ✦ Chicago Botanic Garden

Weep No More

Weep no more, Love.

The pain feels unbearable,

but it soon will lift.

Redbud trees on pond ✦ Spring ✦ The Morton Arboretum

Saturated in Love

I'm saturated in love,
so greatly blessed
with people, pets, and wildlife
to love and be loved by.

Love is a constant,
a raft that rescues me
when waters become turbulent
as well as when calm.

Field of grass ✦ Spring ✦ The Morton Arboretum

God's Time

Wild grass does not grow
by the ticking of a clock.

A human concept,
time is without our control.

We can't speed it up,
slow it down, or stop the hands.

God is the master timekeeper
in all fields and gardens.

Ultra-violet tropical waterlily ✦ Summer ✦ Chicago Botanic Garden

Purple Power

Power of purple.

A blend of the mystical

and the intuitive.

Water fountain ◆ Summer ◆ Cantigny Park

Water Crown

Fountain water crown,

so powerful and regal,

topping off the pond.

Petunias, snapdragons, African daisies ✦ Spring ✦ Cantigny Park

Well-Tended Gardens

Well-tended gardens

lovingly weeded and fed

growing strong and healthy.

Trees near pond ◆ Autumn ◆ The Morton Arboretum

Tree Spirit Speak

Sometimes when I'm near trees
it's as if their spirits speak to me.
They tell me of their history—
stories of endurance
through the seasons,
through the years.

I honor such trees
for their wisdom, fortitude, courage,
and example of graceful aging.

Garden path ✦ Summer ✦ Chicago Botanic Garden

The Journey Continues

This path will end soon,

but the journey continues,

just differently.

About the Author

Mary K. Doyle is an award-winning and best-selling author of twelve books including *Inspired Caregiving: Weekly Morale Builders, Navigating Alzheimer's: 12 Truths about Caring for Your Loved One,* and *The Alzheimer's Spouse: Finding the Grace to Keep the Promise.* She also is a marketing advisor for ACTA Publications and has a Master of Art degree in Pastoral Theology. You can follow Mary's blog at https://midwestmary.com.

Mary is the widow of popular magician Marshall Brodien, who played Wizzo on WGN-TV's *The Bozo Show.* She lives in a far western suburb of Chicago and has three adult children, four grandchildren, and a large circle of well-loved extended family and friends.